W9-CFV-487

MIDLOTHIAN
PUBLIC LIBRARY

Midlothian
Public Library

14701 S. Kenton Ave.
Midlothian, IL 60445

BAKER & TAYLOR

CHINA
AND
JAPAN

MIDLOTHIAN PUBLIC LIBRARY
14701 S. KENTON AVE.
MIDLOTHIAN, IL 60445

Cultures and Costumes Series:

CHINA AND JAPAN

PAULA HAMMOND

MASON CREST PUBLISHERS

www.masoncrest.com

Mason Crest Publishers Inc.
370 Reed Road
Broomall, PA 19008
(866) MCP-BOOK (toll free)
www.masoncrest.com

Copyright © 2003 Amber Books Ltd.

All rights reserved. No part of this publication may be reproduced or transmitted in any form or by any means, electronic or mechanical, including photocopying, recording, taping, or any information storage and retrieval system, without permission in writing from the publisher.

First printing 2002

1 2 3 4 5 6 7 8 9 10

Library of Congress Cataloging-in-Publication Data available

ISBN 1-59084-436-X

Printed and bound in Malaysia

Editorial and design by
Amber Books Ltd.
Bradley's Close
74–77 White Lion Street
London N1 9PF

Project Editor: Marie-Claire Muir
Designer: Hawes Design

Picture Credits:
All pictures courtesy of Amber Books Ltd.

ACKNOWLEDGMENT
For authenticating this book, the Publishers would like to thank
Robert L. Humphrey, Jr., Professor Emeritus of Anthropology,
George Washington University, Washington, D.C.

Contents

China

Japan

China is the third-largest country in the world, with the greatest population and the oldest civilization of any country. Japan is a long chain of mountainous islands off the mainland coast of Asia.

Introduction

Nearly every species in the animal kingdom adapts to changes in the environment. To cope with cold weather, the cat adapts by growing a longer coat of fur, the bear hibernates, and birds migrate to a different climatic zone. Only humans use costume and culture—what they have learned through many generations—to adapt to the environment.

The first humans developed their culture by using spears to hunt the bear, knives and scrapers to skin it, and needles and sinew to turn the hide into a warm coat to insulate their hairless bodies. As time went on, the clothes humans wore became an indicator of cultural and individual differences. Some were clearly developed to be more comfortable in the environment, others were designed for decorative, economic, political, and religious reasons.

Ritual costumes can tell us about the deities, ancestors, and civil and military ranking in a society, while other clothing styles can identify local or national identity. Social class, gender, age, economic status, climate, profession, and political persuasion are also reflected in clothing. Anthropologists have even tied changes in the hemline length of women's dresses to periods of cultural stress or relative calm.

In 13 beautifully illustrated volumes, the *Cultures and Costumes: Symbols of their Period* series explores the remarkable variety of costumes found around the world and through different eras. Each book shows how different societies have clothed themselves, revealing a wealth of diverse and sometimes mystifying explanations. Costume can be used as a social indicator by scientists, artists, cinematographers, historians, and designers—and also provide students with a better understanding of their own and other cultures.

ROBERT L. HUMPHREY, JR., Professor Emeritus of Anthropology,
George Washington University, Washington, D.C.

Ancient China: Early People to First Emperor

"On the banks of a mighty river, there stands an ancient city of great size and splendor. This city is full of fine mansions, inns, and dwelling houses. All the treasures of India—precious stones, pearls, and other rarities—are brought here. So, too, are the choicest and costliest products."

So wrote the 17-year-old Venetian Marco Polo, describing the great Chinese empire to his readers in 13th-century Italy. To Marco, China was an exotic land, full of mystery and excitement, where "gold dust is found in rivers, and vast jungles teem with elephants and unicorns." He and his family were among the very few Westerners to have visited the mighty empire of **Kublai Khan**, and his vivid descriptions gave his readers a small glimpse of an unusually rich and ancient culture.

Until the 1700s, many images of China were still based on descriptions given by Marco Polo, who described Chinese culture, learning, and the flowing, elegant costumes worn by her people.

From Longshan to Zhou

China is a vast country that covers one-fifth of the Asian continent, stretching across deserts, over snow-topped mountains, and **encompassing** more than 55 different ethnic groups in its population. By the time of the fall of the **Roman Empire**, China was already thousands of years old and is still today one of the world's oldest living cultures.

Civilization began in China around 5000–3000 B.C. with a people called the **Yangshao**. The Yangshao lived along the Huang He Valley, which is a wide, fertile area along the banks of the Yellow River. This early Stone Age culture had its own writing system and produced simple but beautiful art, decorated with geometric shapes, flowers, birds, and animals. Around 3300–2200 B.C., settlers called the **Longshan** moved into the region. It is from a blend of these two early civilizations that Chinese culture developed. With it came the rich, flowing, elegant costumes that have come to symbolize Chinese ideas and ideals over the centuries.

The Jade Age

It was the Longshan who gave China its first dynasty, the Shang (ca. 1766–1122 B.C.). Ancient accounts say that the Shang were the second of the legendary Three Dynasties. These Three Dynasties included the Xia (ca. 2205–2198 B.C.) and the

Traditional Chinese robes did not have pockets, so small personal items would generally be carried in pouches, which could be hidden inside a garment's voluminous sleeves.

Zhou (ca. 1122–256 B.C.), which ruled ancient China during a "Jade Age" of progress, peace, and prosperity. Due to the huge time scales involved, much of what we think we know about ancient China is hard to confirm. Until recently, it was believed that the Xia and the Shang existed only in legend. However, discoveries of royal tombs in Anyang, thought to be the Shang capital city, have now offered evidence to support the historical existence of a Jade Age.

One of the most spectacular of these tombs was the grave of Fu Hai, a wife of the Shang king Wu Ding. Fu Hai was a legendary figure, said to have commanded an army of 13,000 warriors in battle against the Qiang tribes. Her grave contained fine ivory carvings, bronze pots, sculptures, and 590 pieces of a green gemstone called jade.

Jade, called *yu* in China, symbolized nobility, immortality, and perfection. The ancient Chinese used it extensively in clothing and headdresses, jewelry, and offerings to the dead. In the Longshan and Shang periods, it was only possible to shape jade by grinding. This process was extremely labor-intensive and required great skill.

A Rich Tradition

Clothing has always been an important means of self-expression in China. In ancient times, a person's wardrobe represented not just wealth and social standing, but also reflected his or her traditions, beliefs, and cultural heritage.

Much of what we know about how the ancient Chinese dressed comes from the remains of clothing found in tombs. The ancient Chinese buried their dead with everything they were thought to need in the afterlife. In the case of some emperors, these "needs" included wives and servants, who were executed and buried as part of the grave goods.

During the Shang and Zhou periods, strict guidelines were drawn up detailing what could be worn by each rank of society. These guidelines became more elaborate with each successive generation—so that by the time of Marco Polo, color, cut, and manufacture of clothing were all rigidly controlled by the

Jade Armor

For the very wealthy, burial suits of jade were made to protect the wearer's body from decay. The jade suit of Liu Sheng, whose father ruled the Han Dynasty (202 B.C.–A.D. 220), was made from over 2,000 pieces of jade, which were sewn together with gold wire. This suit would have taken more than 10 years to make. Despite such elaborate attempts to ward off the deterioration of death, when his grave was opened in 1968, only his suit had survived. Inside his precious armor, Liu Sheng's body was nothing but dust and crushed bone.

state. Clothes found in tombs of the period confirm that, by the time of the early emperors, costume was an important way of indicating rank and social standing. They also testify to the clothes-making skills of the ancient Chinese. Tombs from the Shang era have been found containing beautiful single-color **damask** silks. In later Zhou graves, fine silk **brocades** and **gauzes** have been discovered. These all reflect the elegance and richness of the developing Chinese culture.

Three Costumes, Many Styles

There is no such thing as a typical Chinese costume. Ancient clothing styles varied from region to region, along with the cultures and traditions of the people who wore them. Despite this, traditional Chinese clothes do share certain features: beauty, elegance, and simplicity.

For clarity, most Chinese clothes can be classified as "long robe" or "skirt-and-top" style. These definitions ignore thousands of years of changing fashions, but do make it possible to visualize the basic look of Chinese costume. Three specific garments can be identified as the most traditional: the *ch'ang p'ao*, the *pien-fu*, and the *shen-i*.

Simple clothes of undyed hemp, similar to those shown in this image, were generally worn by the poor. For special occasions, they wore brightly colored regional costumes.

The *ch'ang p'ao* is an ankle-length robe with wide, flowing sleeves. The *pien-fu* is a ceremonial costume that comprises a knee-length tunic, an ankle-length skirt, and a *pien*, which is a cylindrical headdress.

The *shen-i* looks like a coat and skirt, but the two sections are actually sewn together to make a long robe, which is sometimes tied at the waist with a length of silk. *Shen-i* means "deep clothing" because of the generous cut of the cloth.

The Long and Short of It

The length of a person's clothes often indicated his or her social status. A famous story tells of one shopkeeper who divided his customers into two groups: the *chuan chang shande*, meaning "those who wear long clothes," and the *duan yi bang*, which was "the short-clothes group."

Heavy coats and winter woolens were unknown in ancient China. Instead, layers of clothing were added as the weather grew colder and were peeled off again as the summer approached.

Empire, the demand for Chinese silk was so great that it threatened to **bankrupt** the Roman economy. No one knows for sure if the tale of the discovery of silk, around 2700 B.C., is true, but silk was vital to the Chinese economy and was **pivotal** in the development of Chinese costume and culture.

The First Emperor's Army

China's first emperor, Shi Huangdi, was determined that he would be as powerful in death as he had been in life. To protect and support him in the afterlife, over 10,000 lifesized pottery figures were buried with him. This amazing terra cotta army included infantry, cavalry, archers, and charioteers. When newly made, the figures were all armed and painted exactly as an army of the period would have looked.

At the heart of any ancient army was the infantry. Shi Huangdi's terra cotta foot soldiers are simply attired in light hemp tunics and leggings. The tunics were probably padded with cotton wadding or made of treated animal skins to protect the wearer from arrows and spear blows. A few of the figures—possibly officers—are shown in scale-mail jackets. These were worn on top of the tunic and were probably made from small squares of iron or bronze riveted together to form a simple but effective body armor. Scarves worn around the neck protected the wearer from sword blows above the shoulder.

The crossbow was invented by the Chinese around 450 B.C., and the terra cotta army, as would be expected, includes rank upon rank of both archers and crossbowmen. The archers are painted wearing short tunics belted at the waist. The crossbowmen, who would have been considered more valuable than the archers, generally have armor on the upper body, similar to those worn by the officers.

Traces of paint on the terra cotta figures show that they were originally brightly painted, with hats of brown and white tied in place with red sashes. Color had great significance for the Chinese, and this was especially important in battle. During the Warring States period, when Chinese armies from different regions fought for control of the country, enemies would have been easy to identify by the colors that they wore. Armies from different regions wore different colors: black for the north, green for the east, red for the west, and white for the south. A battlefield in those days was a very colorful place.

Killer Fashions

The figures in the terra cotta army were originally fully armed. One particularly impressive figure carried a sword almost 35 inches (88 cm) long. Although some historians think that the figure's great height— 6 feet 6 inches (over 2 m)—merely symbolized his importance, the sword he carries is actually a fashionable length for the period. One account of an attempt to assassinate Shi Huangdi describes how the emperor could not defend himself because his sword was too long to draw from its **scabbard**.

Imperial Court and the Ruling Classes

By the end of the Zhou Dynasty, around 256 B.C., China already had a history that spanned several thousand years, during which it saw the development of writing, philosophy, an efficient system of government and law, and rich traditions in art, architecture, and costume.

The history of imperial China deals with an equally colossal period of time—from the Qin Dynasty, which united the country under its first emperor in 221 B.C., to the Qing Dynasty, which was ultimately overthrown by republicans in 1912. Nowhere is this long and complex history better reflected than in the costumes and clothing that the people wore.

Members of the Chinese ruling class and their administrators wore elaborately decorated silk gowns called dragon robes, because of the dragon motifs that decorated them. Wealthy women were not required to wear dragon robes, but often did to show their husband's status.

The Bottom of the Pyramid

Imperial China had a social **hierarchy** based on the teachings of the Chinese philosopher Confucius. Confucius valued hard work, learning, and honesty in public and private life. His "Golden Rule" was, "What you do not wish for yourself, do not do to others."

The spread of Confucianism began around 300 B.C., and the philosophy had become a major influence on Chinese thought by the time of the first Qin emperor. The leaders of the Qin Dynasty (221–206 B.C.) believed in the need for clear rules and leadership, and they laid down a series of laws governing every aspect of life.

This Season's Colors

Fashions in imperial China often changed as quickly as fashions do today. In the 1760s, sky blue was replaced by rose pink as the season's most to-be-seen-in color. In the 1780s, a battle-weary general called Fukang'an started a craze for bright red that came to be known as "Fu red." By the 1800s, yellow and pale gray had become the new must-have shades. This passion for fashion created some unlikely trendsetters.

These rules depended on a strict social hierarchy. At the top of the pyramid was the emperor and members of the imperial household. Next were scholars, then peasants, who were valued because the country depended on them for food. Below them were the artisans, who produced the goods needed by the people. At the bottom of China's social pyramid were merchants. According to Confucians, merchants had no value to society because they produced nothing of worth—becoming wealthy by trading on the skills of others and by selling luxury items that no one really needed.

Trade and Industry

For many centuries, trade in China was controlled by the emperor. Key goods were state-produced—especially silk, which, after the mid-17th century, was controlled by the Weaving and Dying Office. Trade opportunities were few, and

Beautifully decorated silk umbrellas existed in China at least 2,000 years ago. Aside from being practical, parasols were used by dancers and acrobats as part of their performances.

China's **antipathy** to the outside world made life very difficult for merchants who traded with foreigners. Despite this, merchants did become extremely prosperous, and they enjoyed displaying their success by wearing elaborate and costly clothing.

In 199 B.C., an imperial **edict** attempted to put merchants "back in their place" by banning them from wearing silk, carrying arms, and riding horses—all things traditionally associated with the nobility. It was only in the 19th century that these restrictions were relaxed, because the merchants' money was needed to help fight antigovernment factions. In some regions, merchants were even allowed to buy silk dragon robes of the style worn by government officials. These robes boosted the merchants' social standing and were worn with pride.

Scholars and Public Servants

The complex task of managing and legislating for such a vast empire required an efficient civil service. Initially, administrators were chosen from ruling families, but by the time of the Tang Dynasty (A.D. 618–907), an elaborate system of examinations ensured that only the most capable were chosen for

Women in Imperial China

As in many cultures, the roles of men and women in ancient China were strictly regulated. In Confucian philosophy, women were expected to be good daughters, respectful wives, and efficient managers of the home. Men were brought up to be rulers and providers.

In the Confucian *Book of Rites*, written in the second century A.D., an ideal for the world was outlined in which "men manage the outer, women manage the inner." Within this strictly stratified society, women were encouraged to "work diligently with their hands." Men, Confucian philosophy declared, "should plow and women weave." The Chinese word for womanly work—*nügong*—included not just weaving, but also embroidery, spinning, sewing, shoemaking, and sericulture (the raising of silkworms).

Much of this *nügong* was done in the home, but employment for women was also provided by state-run workshops. As the centuries progressed, it

Wealthy Chinese women were carefully groomed. Hairstyles could be particularly elaborate, with strips of bamboo used to tease the hair into elaborate shapes. Fresh flowers and feathers were also popular and could be used in the hair to create a pleasing design.

became increasingly acceptable for women to add to the family income in this way. By 1881, there were over 1,000 women working in the imperial silk workshop in Suzhou. Although wealthy women never made their own clothing or worked in the state-run factories, they were nevertheless still encouraged to develop the necessary skills. In the famous *Story of the Stone*, written around 1760, the family **matriarch** tells her granddaughters, "We will never need to do our own sewing…But it's well to know how. Then you will never need to be at the mercy of others."

Lotus Shoes

In 1975, archaeologists made a fascinating discovery. While digging in an area on China's southern coast, they uncovered the tomb of Lady Huang, a noble of the Song Dynasty (A.D. 960–1279). In it were six pairs of beautifully preserved hemp shoes, edged with delicate blossom motifs and silk ribbon. The average

Women's Work, Men's Work

During China's imperial period, Chinese shoes came in many styles, depending on the wealth of the wearer and the region that he or she lived in. For simplicity, these can be described as outdoor and indoor shoes. Unlike shoes in the West, which were usually made from leather, both indoor and outdoor shoes were made from hemp, with decorated silken uppers. For indoor shoes, which resembled slippers, soles were stiffened by spreading thick layers of rice paste onto the material. Indoor shoes were made by women. Outdoor shoes were men's work, because they had wooden soles that required the skills of a carpenter.

In the 19th and early 20th centuries, unmarried Han women wore their hair long and simply dressed with fresh flowers. Married women preferred the "round-head" style shown here.

size of these shoes was around five inches (13 cm). These tiny shoes are believed to be the earliest evidence of the practice of foot-binding.

Foot-binding involved tying a young girl's feet with lengths of cloth to restrict growth. It was an extremely painful process, which buckled the arch of the foot to give it a clubbed appearance. This early form of "cosmetic surgery" probably began in the imperial court. The bound feet forced women to walk slowly, with small, dainty steps, and over the centuries, small feet came to symbolize beauty and modesty. Eventually, small feet became desirable attributes for a woman to have—without them she could not expect to marry to her best advantage.

Foot-binding occurred when a girl came of age, which was considered to be around seven years old. Because foot-binding meant losing a valuable worker, poorer families would delay binding as long as possible.

The foot-binding ritual began by preparing the foot with medicinal herbs to soften the bones and aid healing. Depending on the region, feet would be expected not only to be small, but also narrow or with toes that pointed or curled up at the end. By binding the prepared foot tightly in lengths of freshly woven cloth some 4 inches wide by 13 feet long (10 cm by 4 m), it was hoped to achieve the desired fashionable shape. The process could take many months, requiring special training shoes of progressively smaller and smaller size. Once the foot was bound, it could not be unbound without causing great pain, so even in bed a Chinese woman would wear special sock-like sleeping shoes.

The tradition of foot-binding eventually attracted the attention of reformers, who felt that it was a cruel and unnecessary practice. However, in some rural regions, such as Yunnan, it remained a common tradition until the 1950s. Only a determined campaign by the Communist Party stopped foot-binding completely.

Amethyst and Amber

Fashion was one of the few areas in which women in imperial China enjoyed greater freedom than men. While male costume was regulated by the Board of Rites, which designated styles for each year, wealthy women could not hold public office and so were not restricted to wearing official robes.

Wealthy, fashionable women in imperial China enjoyed expensive fabrics, jewelry, and ornamentation, but always remained aware of the main **precepts** of style—simplicity and elegance. Mrs. Archibald Little, writing in *Intimate China*, recalled a roomful of charmingly dressed Chinese ladies: "the exquisite gradations of color of their embroidered skirts and jackets, the brilliancy of the

Stepping into Eternity

When a Chinese woman reached the age of 49, she was free to hand over her household chores to someone else and spend what remained of her "old age" pursuing hobbies and interests. The one final task that she had to do was to make her own funeral shoes. These were called "longevity shoes," and a woman would expect to take them into the afterlife with her.

Walking any distance with bound feet was difficult and required women to walk slowly, with small steps. These women are taking advantage of a simple form of sedan chair to move around more easily.

head ornaments, and their rouge…Their skirts…[were] prettily made…in a succession of tiny pleats…only loosely fastened over the hips, so as to feather [a]round the feet when they move."

The ladies Mrs. Little describes were probably wealthy descendants of the Han Dynasty. The skirts they wore were called *yu lin bai zhe qun*, which means "fish-scale, 100-pleat skirts." Such skirts were made from highly embroidered satin and decorated with images from nature, such as plum blossoms,

A selection of Chinese accessories from the Qing Dynasty includes a drawstring pouch for holding snuff (bottom left), glasses (top), and earrings (bottom right).

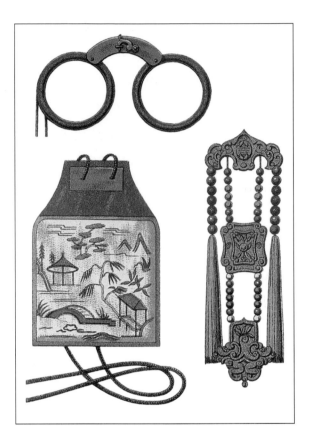

chrysanthemums, and narcissi. Fish-scale skirts were generally worn under a three-quarter-length robe, and were popular with younger Han women during the 1800s.

Manchu women, who belonged to the ruling Qing Dynasty, were an equally impressive sight. As Lady Hosie describes in her memoirs, *Two Gentlemen of China*: "Their long straight gowns fell to the ankles without a break in a shimmer of exquisite thick satin …amethyst, aquamarine, and amber." These spectacular garments were called *qi pao*, meaning "banner robes," and were part of every fashionable Manchu lady's wardrobe.

Rouge, Flowers, and a Little White Lead

Hairstyle and makeup were a vital part of a woman's costume in imperial China. For the wealthy especially, hair styling could take many hours and would need the assistance of at least one maid to achieve the desired effect.

While poorer women were content simply to pin up or braid their hair, followers of fashion opted for lavish styles with quirky descriptive names such as "magpie tail" and "falling from a horse." The most complex styles would be set in place by a resin obtained by soaking wood chippings in water. This served as an early form of hair laquer, and set the hair solidly in place.

Once the hair was dressed, makeup was applied. During the 17th century, this could be hazardous, because face powder contained a number of toxic substances, including white lead, which damaged the skin. Ladies of the ruling Qing Dynasty applied this powder in thick layers to give the face a smooth, white, masklike appearance, and red dye was then applied to the cheeks, and thin eyebrows drawn onto the forehead. Lips were painted to look small and round. Red dye made from alum and balsam-flower leaves was also applied to nails.

Foreign Influences

China's relations with the West had always been difficult. Christian missionaries from Europe had spent centuries trying to convert them from Buddhism. Dutch and English merchants had tried over and over to gain control of the silk trade. Finally, in 1839, war broke out with Britain. The conflict was, on the surface, a dispute over the illegal importation of opium into China. However, it was in reality a trade war. While fashionable Europeans cried out for Chinese silk, pottery, and furnishings, China had no need of European goods. By selling opium, Western merchants had finally found something that the Chinese people wanted—and were prepared to trade for. After three years of fighting, the British eventually agreed to stop the trade in opium in exchange for generous trade treaties for Britain and her allies.

Although initially resented by the Chinese, these new trade agreements led to a growing interest in European goods and ideas. This was particularly noticeable in fashion. By the late 19th century, the long, freely flowing clothing that had been worn for centuries by Chinese women began to reflect the growing influence of European styles. Clothing called ***cheong sam*** developed, adapting elements of European dress to suit traditional Chinese styles. *Cheong sam* featured close-fitting trousers and short, tailored jackets with high collars, and emphasized the shape of the body in a way that traditional long robes did not. In Europe, the same cross-cultural exchange was taking place, with women copying Chinese styling to give their clothing a more **Oriental** feel.

Ancient Japan and the Ainu

Japan is an island nation whose early culture owes much to the influence of the Chinese. Under the rule of Prince Shotoku (A.D. 593–622), Japan adopted and adapted many Chinese ideas—about writing, philosophy, ways of governing, and ideals of beauty in clothing and ornamentation.

However, it would be wrong to see Japan simply as a group of small islands imitating its larger mainland neighbor. Both nations have a wealth of traditions rooted in thousands of years of history, a history reflected in the styling and beauty of Chinese and Japanese costume.

Source of the Sun

The ancient Chinese called their nation *zhangguo*, which means "middle kingdom," because they believed that their country was at the center of the world. They had an equally **momentous** name for the islands to the east of their mainland home. Because it appeared that the sun rose from behind these islands

Traditional images that have come to be associated with Japan: the kimono, a samurai warrior with a shaved head and sword, fans, and the samisen, which is a Japanese stringed instrument.

every morning, they called them *ji ping*. The Japanese used the same phrase, which they pronounced Nippon or Nihon, meaning "source of the sun."

Japan is made up of a collection of islands that curve for almost 1,200 miles (1,900 km) across the northern Pacific Ocean. Most of Japan has a mountainous terrain, with volcanoes, such as Mount Fuji, forming part of the nation's spectacular natural beauty.

The Ainu

Modern Japan contains many different ethnic groups, including Koreans, Chinese, and the Ainu. The Ainu, who form one of Japan's largest minority groups, are very different from the Japanese in appearance, culture, and beliefs. The **Ainu** are considered the **aboriginal** people of Japan, and their traditions give a unique insight into the country's early culture.

Ainu means "human." No one knows where the Ainu originally came from, but because their beliefs show strong ties with nature, it is likely that they are descended from an early hunter-gatherer culture. It is believed that the Ainu may have settled in Japan as long as 10,000 years ago. The height of Ainu civilization occurred during the 13th and 14th centuries A.D. It was during this time that the Ainu came into conflict with Japanese settlers, who occupied their land and imposed their own culture and traditions on them. Like many aboriginal peoples, the Ainu have only recently begun to have their rights, language, and traditions recognized and protected by law.

Birds, Bark, and Cotton

The Ainu love of nature can be seen most clearly in their traditional costumes. Early Ainu clothing consisted of a knee-length robe, with wide sleeves that reached the wearer's elbow. This robe was tied at the waist and often worn with other layers on top. The Ainu used natural materials to make and decorate their clothing. These included bird skin, fish skin, animal hide, wild rye, and bark. Bark clothes were not actually made from bark, but from fibers stripped from

The fan originated in Japan around A.D. 700. It was quickly adopted by the Chinese and later became fashionable in Europe when Dutch traders started to export them.

the inner part of tree roots and branches. These types of clothes are called **attush** and are still worn by the Ainu today.

Retarpe, which means "white things," is a type of *attush* made from nettles, which give the cloth its traditional white color. Most *attush* are plain, although elaborate designs are added to clothing worn on special occasions, using a technique known as appliqué. Appliqué involves applying decoration by sewing a smaller piece of material onto a larger piece to create the desired effect.

Later, as the Ainu began to trade with the Japanese, they started to use cotton, which they decorated with elaborate and brightly colored embroidery. These clothes were called *chikarkarpe* ("the things we embroider").

Growing Up the Ainu Way

The Ainu were a deeply spiritual people who believed absolutely in the power of demons and spirits to inflict harm on the living. When an Ainu child was born, it was given a temporary name, which was intended to ward off the

Crown of Twigs

On special occasions, Ainu men would wear a crown called a *sapanpe*. Made from an elaborate arrangement of twigs and wood shavings, it rested precariously on the head. Carved figures, which represented animal spirits, were used to decorate the center of the *sapanpe*.

demon of ill health. Such names included *poyshi*, which means "small excrement," and *shion*, meaning "old excrement." Old or secondhand clothing was used to make children's clothes. This, too, was intended to ward off demons of illness, who were believed to hate worn-out things.

Ainu children wore plain *attush* robes until they came of age, which was around 15 years old. At this point, males were finally allowed to dress as adults—to wear loincloths and patterned *attush* and to dress their hair. For girls, approaching adulthood was marked by tattoos on their lips, hands, and arms. This lengthy process began at the age of 12 and, once completed, at the age of 16 or 17, it was a sign that a girl was ready for marriage.

Costume continued to be important throughout an Ainu's life. While courting, couples would exchange gifts of clothing, leggings, and embroidered cloth. During pregnancy, a maternity belt, made symbolically from a husband's loincloth, was worn. Ainu culture was based on a series of rituals that were intended to guide a person through one life and into the next. The Ainu believed that, at death, the spirit returned to its own world, where it would wait to be reborn. Clothes were used to mark significant life events in this never-ending cycle of death and rebirth.

Early Roots

Many **anthropologists** believe that modern-day Japanese people are descended from several groups of settlers who came to the islands over a period of several thousands of years. The first of these groups was called the **Jōmon**. The Jōmon settled along the coasts of Japan's larger islands—Hokkaido, Honshu, Kyushu, and Shikoku—around 4500 B.C. Jōmon means "cord pattern," the name given to the style of decoration found on ancient pottery from this period. Over the centuries, the Jōmon were gradually pushed out of their coastal lands by two new waves of settlers. One group settled in Kyushu, the other, the **Yayoi**, settled on Honshu around 200 B.C. The Yayoi are named after an area of modern Tokyo where the remains of their civilization have been found. Most modern Japanese are descended from the Yayoi.

For the poor, clothing remained virtually unchanged for many centuries. Versions of these simple, loose, undyed clothes were worn through much of Japan's history and were ideal garments for manual work.

A cross-section of Japanese society in the mid-1800s, before the arrival of European fashions: the women wear long robes with traveling jackets, and the man's leggings and short top are designed to allow easy movement.

Early Clothing

It is believed that the Jōmon were originally nomads from Asia—and, from what little we know about how they dressed, their clothing seems more suited to a life on the mainland than in the hot, damp, mountainous regions of Japan. Their clothes—tight trousers and short tunic tops—would be ideal for hunter-gatherer nomads, but not for farmers, who needed loose clothing to move around in.

In contrast, the Yayoi seem much better adapted to life in ancient Japan. In a Chinese document from the third century A.D., the *Wei Chih*, early Yayoi men are described as wearing unsewn fabric wrapped around the body. Women wore equally basic garments. These were made from a piece of cloth folded over the body with a hole cut for the head, a little like a modern-day poncho. Such simple clothes would probably have been made on a backstrap loom. This was an early form of loom that produced lengths of cloth approximately the same width as the weaver's body. To produce a robe, two lengths of cloth would be sewn together at the shoulders and belted at the middle. The sides were often left unsewn.

The Birth of a Nation

When people have to struggle to survive, clothing becomes just another necessity—it does not matter what cut or color a garment is as long as it keeps you warm. As civilizations develop and technology improves, so that more food is grown with less effort, clothing becomes more important. Clothes become a way for societies to express their identity, to demonstrate their artistic skills, and—over time—to reflect the ideals of the developing culture. The early Yayoi were farmers and hunters. They grew rice and worked with basic tools of stone and iron to produce the things they needed. Their simple garments were designed to be practical and durable. It was only once the collection of small Yayoi villages grew into a **confederation** of chiefdoms that art and culture started to flourish.

The formation of a Japanese state brought the development of distinct styles of art and costume. This included the development of a form of pottery called *haniwa. Haniwa* sculptures date from between A.D. 200 and 500, and have been found in large numbers in the elaborate, key-shaped tombs of the period. *Haniwa* figures represent animals, houses, and people from all sections of society: soldiers, nobles, holy men, and farmers. These figures show a people who appreciated costume and jewelry. In the images of both men and women are closely tailored jackets that open down the front. Under this, men wear long, baggy trousers. Women wear flowing, pleated skirts called *mo.* Jewelry is big and bold, with round necklaces and earrings found on many of the female figures.

Clearly, by this period, clothes had become much more than just the "unsewn" pieces of cloth that are described in the Chinese *Wei Chih.* They were garments designed for beauty, as well as practicality, and showed the emergence of Japan's unique style of costume.

"Things to Wear"

A kimono—literally a "thing (*mono*) to wear (*ki*)"—is a long, flowing garment with wide sleeves, tied around the waist with a sash called an *obi* and worn by both men and women. The kimono is probably one of the world's simplest, most elegant and sophisticated national costumes.

This Japanese style of dress has Chinese roots. Prince Shotoku (A.D. 593–622) was a charismatic and intelligent leader, famed for his learning and his prophetic dreams, which guided his decision-making. Shotoku was a devout Buddhist and was determined to build Japan into a Buddhist nation following the model developed by the Han Dynasty in China. From their example, Shotoku adopted Chinese models of government that aimed to bring peace, stability, and unity to the country.

It was during the period of his Taika Reforms that Chinese styles of dress first started to be worn in the Japanese imperial court. Following the Chinese example, society was classified into ranks, with each rank distinguished by the color and style of its dress. These garments clearly reflect their Chinese roots, with layers of long, loose robes tied at the waist with a sash.

In A.D. 858, power in Japan effectively moved from the emperor to the powerful Fujiwara family. This shift in power was a key feature of the Heian

These women are dressed in the *koshi-maki* style. In summer, the long outer robe was tied at the waist and worn off the shoulders so that it trailed on the floor.

There are over 300 ways of correctly tying an *obi*. Each method has its own name, such as "drum bow" or "shellfish bow," which describes the shape of the knot. These images shows the *obi*'s elegance and beauty.

kimonos were worn longer, with hems that trailed behind the wearers as they walked. Women of the imperial court wore robes called *sōkutai*, with huge, open-ended sleeves called *osode*, which were an extravagant example of this style.

As the power of the emperor decreased, however, fashions started to become more practical. Kimonos remained long, but began to be worn gathered up at the waist, with drawstring cuffs that could be pulled closed. An example of this can be seen in the *kariginu*, a practical garment for horseback riding. The drawstrings allowed the wearer to close up the sleeves and keep them out of the way when drawing a bow. During the Edo-Tokugawa (A.D. 1600–1853) and

A traveling priest (left) wears white split-toed socks called *tabi*, with *zōri* sandals. The samurai man, on the right, wears *geta*, which are sandals with a raised wooden sole.

Kamakura (A.D. 1185–1333) periods, the warrior class, called **samurai**, became Japan's leaders in all but title. Under their influence, Japanese costume became less showy and more functional. It is from the samurai style of clothes that modern-day kimonos developed.

Oil and Water

Fire was a constant threat during the Edo-Tokugawa Period. By this time, Japanese cities were huge. Houses were made of wood and paper, and oil lamps and wood-burning cooking stoves provided the only forms of light and heat. For safety, every district had its own fire department, which could be identified by the flag it carried. Firemen were renowned for their insane bravery, and their heroism became the subject of popular legend.

Wearing hooded jackets made of layers of thick, quilted cotton, firemen would be doused in water before entering a burning building. Their robes were designed to soak up as much water as possible. This, it was hoped, would keep the firefighter cool enough to get close to the flames. When firefighters were off-duty, these robes were reversible, with fire-resistant decorations painted on the inside.

The Power of the Samurai

The fight had been hard. Tomoe Gozen took a deep breath and looked around at the battlefield. There were just four of her comrades left now, and Tomoe knew that death must be near. With one last effort, she spurred her horse forward, toward the eastern provinces—and safety.

No one knows for sure if Tomoe Gozen made it to safety or died on the battlefield at Awazu. As a samurai, Tomoe would have been expected to fight and, if necessary, to die for her lord. "The way of the samurai," wrote a warrior of the Nabeshima clan, "can be found in death." However, the name samurai refers not just to fierce and resolute warriors such as Tomoe, but also to an entire section of Japanese society—whether they knew how to use a sword or not.

Birth of the Samurai

During the ninth century A.D., the power of the Japanese emperor began to wane, and the Fujiwara family effectively seized control of the imperial court.

Samurai helmets were often topped with elaborate designs made from papier-mâché and lacquer on a wooden frame. Full face masks were rarely worn in battle because they restricted vision.

Samurai armor is probably among the most instantly recognizable items of military clothing in the world, and strict rules outlined every detail of dress. This included the order in which items were put on.

First on, of course, was the underwear. A long loincloth of cotton or linen was wrapped between the legs, pulled up under the chin, and tied in place around the neck like a bib. On top of this would be a short kimono and *hakama*. A *hakama* was a long, pleated, open-sided skirt that looked a little like

When You've Got to Go...

Although elaborate, samurai armor was also designed to deal with the practicalities of life. The *hakama* had an open crotch so that, in emergencies, a samurai could easily loosen the loincloth and relieve himself without having to leave the battlefield.

This image shows a samurai putting on the layers of his armor. In addition to a sword, the samurai carries a *yumi*, which was a bow drawn using the thumb and forefinger rather than thumb and three fingers, which was the technique used by European archers.

trousers. Next came the outer robe, leggings, and boots.

After this came the armor, which was put on from bottom to top and from right to left across the body. Samurai armor was made of leather and metal, which was lacquered to give added protection to the wearer. Early armor was black, with brightly colored laces holding the lacquered strips in place. Later, deep red or rich brown lacquer was used. In contrast to modern military clothing, which is intended to help soldiers blend into the background, samurai armor was designed to intimidate the enemy and help the wearer stand out on the battlefield—and boost his fame. Weaponry, helmet, and face armor completed the outfit.

Nō

Nō theater developed in the Muromachi Period (A.D. 1333–1568) and, by the 1700s, was the preferred form of entertainment of the samurai class. Nō deals with epic themes: civil war (Shura Nō), human tragedy (Zatsu Nō), love (Kazura Nō), gods (Kami Nō), and supernatural beings (Kichiku Nō). Like Kabuki, Nō costumes were elaborate and were often handed down through the actor's family from generation to generation.

In Nō, all the roles are played by men, who wear masks during the performance. These masks are neutral in expression, but are designed to convey difficult ideas or emotions to the audience. These complex ideas are called *yūgen*. *Yūgen* was explained by the Buddhist poet Shōetsu as those thoughts and emotions that "lie within the mind...it may be suggested by the veil of a cloud over the moon, or by the mists of autumn on the mountainside."

Each of the five types of Nō has masks that represent characters the audience would expect to recognize. These masks can be spectacular—the mask

Netsuke and *Inro*

Traditional Japanese clothing does not have pockets. Instead, everyday items were carried in small, exquisitely designed boxes called *inro*. *Inro* became popular during the Edo-Tokugawa Period (A.D. 1600–1853) and are an example of lacquerwear. Lacquer is a thick resin that comes from trees that grow in China. Objects coated with lacquer are not simply beautiful, but also waterproof and heat-resistant. *Inro* were attached to the *obi* by a cord that was held in place by *netsuke*, which are miniature carved beads generally made from wood or ivory. Although most *netsuke* are no bigger than a thumb, they feature intricately carved scenes of animals, fish, gods, and drunken spirits called *shojo*.

A feudal system of government meant that the military was highly regarded and traditional weaponry, such as two-handed swords and mail coats, was, until recently, used alongside more modern equipment.

of the god Arashiyama, for example, is gold with large metallic eyes, gaping mouth, and long, lolling tongue. Ikazuchi, a fierce demon, has a red serpent-like face, fangs, and bulging golden eyes.

No grew out of Shinto and Buddhist rites, and is still a popular form of theater today, reminding its audience of the beauty and wealth of Japan's long and complex history.

Glossary

Note: Specialized words relating to clothing are explained within the text.
For easy reference, words that appear more than once are listed below.

Aboriginal living in a place from the earliest time

Ainu Japan's aboriginal people

Anthropologist someone who studies human origins, characteristics
and beliefs

Antipathy dislike or hostility

Attush Ainu clothing made from woven bark fibers

Bankrupt to be in a state of financial ruin

Brocade generally silk fabrics with a raised pattern

Chao fu court robe worn by a Chinese emperor and occasionally officials

Cheong sam a long robe designed to emphasise the shape of the body

Confederation a loose alliance of people

Coronet an ornamental wreath or band for the head

Edict a law

Damask reversible silk or linen fabric with a woven pattern

Encompass to include

Gauze thin, transparent cloth used for Japanese veils

Haiku Japanese poem containing 17 syllables

Hakama samurai short, pleated, open-sided skirt that looked a little like
trousers

Hierarchy any group arranged in a specific order, usually relating to status

Jōmon early civilization that settled in Japan around 4500 B.C

Kabuki Japanese theater featuring elaborate costumes and stylized movements

Kimono flowing robe worn in Japan

Kublai Khan (1216–1294) founder of the Mongol Dynasty, which ruled
China from A.D. 1279

Long pao Chinese robes worn by government or court officials; also called dragon robes

Longshan (3300–2200 B.C.). second civilization of the Huang He Valley; with the Yangshao, it evolved into ancient Chinese civilization

Mandarin Chinese administrator-scholar (called *guan* in Chinese) employed by the state

Matriarch female leader or the most respected female member of a family

Meritorious worthy of praise

Momentous grand

Motif a repeating theme

Obi sash that ties a kimono

Oriental relating to eastern Asia

Parasol type of umbrella used to keep off the sun instead of rain

Pivotal vitally important

Precepts guides or rules

Roman Empire according to legend, founded in 753 B.C.; fell to invaders in A.D. 476

Samurai Japanese warrior class

Scabbard holder for a sharp-edged weapon, such as a sword

Yangshao (5000–3000 B.C.) first Chinese civilization of the Huang He Valley; see also Longshan

Yayoi people who settled in Japan around 300 B.C., ancestors of the modern Japanese

Chinese Dynasties

ca. 2205–2198 B.C.	Xia becomes the first of the legendary "Three Dynasties."
ca. 1766–1122	Shang era.
ca. 1122–256	Zhou era.
221–206	Qin Dynasty rules a united China.
202 B.C.–A.D. 220	Culture flourishes under the Han Dynasty.
581–618	China is reunified under the Sui Dynasty.
618–907	Tang Dynasty.
960–1279	Song Dynasty.
1279–1368	Mongols conquer China; Marco Polo visits.
1368–1644	Ming Dynasty.
1644–1912	Manchus conquer China and rule as the Qing Dynasty.
1912	China becomes a republic.
1937–1945	Japan invades China; World War II.
1949	Communist People's Republic of China is established.

Japanese Eras

660 B.C.	Founding of Japan under Emperor Jimmu.
A.D. 552–710	Askuka Period.
710–794	Nara Period is dominated by Chinese ideas.
794–1185	Heian Period; the growth of a Japanese national identity.
1185–1333	Kamakura Period begins under Yoritomo as shogun.
1333–1568	Muromachi Period; first Europeans arrive in Japan.
1568–1600	Momoyama Period.
1600–1853	Edo-Tokugawa Period; Europeans expelled from Japan.
1853–1868	U.S. envoy demands trade rights; period of transition.
1868–1912	Meiji Period; Japan becomes industrialized.
1937–1945	World War II; Japan invades China and bombs Pearl Harbor.
1945–1947	Japan is defeated; a democratic constitution is established.

Online Sources

The China Experience
www.chinavista.com/experience
A detailed online index of Web sites dealing with Chinese history, art, culture, and costume. For easy reference, links are broken down into subject areas. Regularly updated.

Chinese Art
www.chinese-art.com
A monthly e-zine for students and anyone interested in Chinese culture and history. Reviews of forthcoming exhibitions that may be of interest to students and teachers.

Destiny: The Culture of China
library.thinkquest.org/70443/culture.html
This easy-to-use site deals with all aspects of Chinese life, old and new. A useful starting point for further study.

The Samurai Archives
www.samurai.archives.com
An excellent site with useful links, FAQs, and an online chat room for sharing ideas or posting queries.

Further Reading

Chunsheng, Li., et al. *China's Minority Peoples.* Beijing: China Pictorial Publishing House, 1995.

Editors at Time-Life Books. *What Life Was Like: In the Land of the Dragon.* Alexandria, VA: Time-Life Books, 1998.

Hucker, Charles. O. *China's Imperial Past.* Stanford: Stanford University Press, 1994.

Latham, Ronald. *The Travels of Marco Polo.* London: Folio Society, 1997.

Martin, Peter. *The Chrysanthemum Throne.* Gloucestershire: Sutton, 1997.

Olson, Kay Melchisedech. *China (Many Cultures, One World).* Minn: Capstone Press, 2003.

Paludan, Ann. *Chronicle of the Chinese Emperors.* London: Thames and Hudson, 1998.

Peers, Christopher and McBride, Angus. *Ancient Chinese Armies: 15,000–200 B.C.*: Oxford: Osprey Military, 1996.

Shelley, Rex. *Japan (Cultures of the World).* New York: Marshall Cavendish, 2001.

Spence, Jonathan and Annping Chin. *The Chinese Century.* London: Harper Collins, 1996.

Westwell, Ian and Nick Grant. *Warriors.* Kent: Grange Books, 1999.

Wilson, Verity. *Chinese Dress.* London: Victoria and Albert Museum, 2001.

About the Author

Paula Hammond was born and educated in the ancient Roman town of Chester, England. After completing a degree in History, Literature, and Theology at Trinity College, she moved to London to pursue a career in publishing. Her writing credits include *Communication Through The Ages*, which traces the history of writing and communication, and *The Grubbiest* *Adventure...Ever*, a project-based research resource for young children. She is currently writing a series for teenagers on notable historical figures and events.

Index